HOW TO GO TO HELL

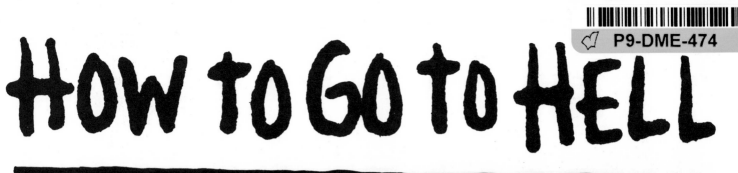

A CARTOON BOOK BY MATT GROENING

OTHER BOOKS BY THIS VERY SAME CARTOONIST

LOVE IS HELL
WORK IS HELL
SCHOOL IS HELL
CHILDHOOD IS HELL
AKBAR & JEFF'S GUIDE TO LIFE
THE BIG BOOK OF HELL

WORKS IN PROGRESS

HOW TO DRESS THE AKBAR & JEFF WAY
HOW TO DANCE THE AKBAR & JEFF WAY
HOW TO WRESTLE THE AKBAR & JEFF WAY
HOW TO STARE AT EACH OTHER THE AKBAR & JEFF WAY
HOW TO FIND YOUR AKBAR IN A WORLD FULL OF JEFFS

FIRST EDITION

COVER DESIGN: MILI SMYTHE

SPECIAL THANKS TO: DIANE PIRRITINO, SONDRA ROBINSON, GARY BUSHERT, MARK GATEWOOD, EILEEN CAMPION, KEITH MAYERSON, SUSAN GRODE, AND THE RADIANT DEBORAH CAPLAN

DEDICATED TO WENDY WOLF, DESPITE DEADLINES AND DEATH THREATS.

LYNDA BARRY IS FUNK QUEEN OF--AH, THE HELL WITH IT.

ISBN 0-06-096879-6

91 92 93 94 95 RRD 10 9 8 7 6 5 4 3 2

HarperPerennial
A Division of HarperCollinsPublishers

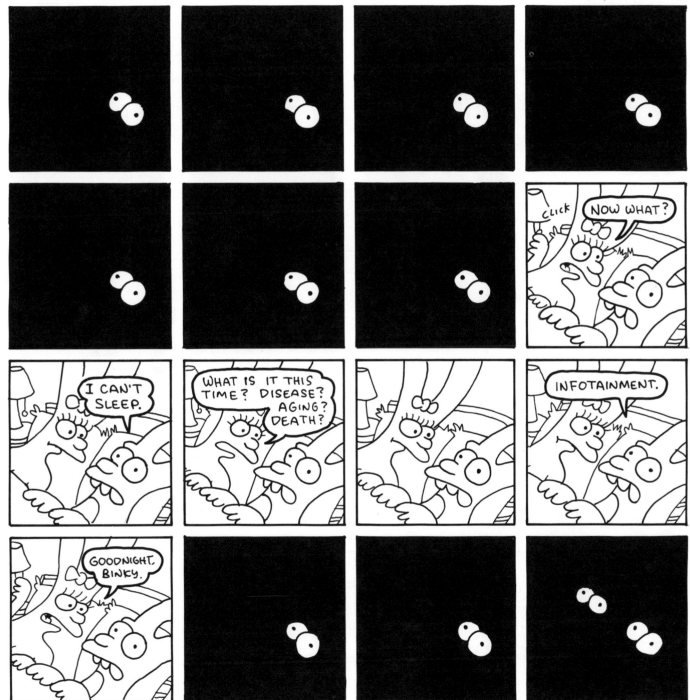

LIFE IN HELL

FORBIDDEN WORDS OF THE 1990s

A-LIST
AUTO SHADE
BABY BOOMER
BATMAN
BETAMAX
BICOASTAL
BIG CHILL GENERATION
BIMBO
BOOMBOX
CALIFORNIA RAISINS
CAREERIST
CASSINGLE
CELEBUTANTE
CELLULITE
CHIC
CHILL OUT
CLAYMATION
COCOONING
CODEPENDENCY
CONCEPTUAL
CROISSANDWICH
CYBERPUNK
DANCERCIZE
DEF
DICEY
D.I.N.K.
DIRTY DANCING
DON'T WORRY, BE HAPPY

DRAMEDY
DRUG KINGPIN
DRY BEER
DUDE
DWEEB
ECLECTIC
ELECTROFUNK
EVIL EMPIRE
FOXY
GET WITH THE PROGRAM
GLITZ
GO FOR IT
GORBY
G-SPOT
GRAPHIC NOVEL
HAPPENIN'
HEADBANGER
HIGH CONCEPT
HOMEBOY
HYPERTEXT
HYPER ANYTHING
ILLIN'
INFOTAINMENT
INTERFACE
JAZZERCIZE
JUST SAY NO
KINDER, GENTLER NATION
LIFE'S A BEACH

LIFESTYLE
LIFESTYLES OF THE RICH AND FAMOUS
LIPOSUCTION
LITE BEER
LOTTO
MAKE MY DAY
MALE BONDING
METALHEAD
MINDSET
MINIMALISM
MINIMALL
MINISTORAGE
MOMMY TRACK
NEO-GEO
NEO ANYTHING
NERD
NETWORKING
NEW AGE
NEW WAVE
NEW ANYTHING
NINJA
NUTRASWEET
OUTRAGEOUS
PALIMONY
PASSIVE-AGGRESSIVE
PEACEKEEPER MISSILE
PEOPLE METER

PETER PAN SYNDROME
PICTIONARY
POLITICALLY CORRECT
POSTMODERN
POSTPUNK
POWER BREAKFAST
POWER LUNCH
QUALITY TIME
RAD
RAMBO
READ MY LIPS
REAGANITE
REFUSENIK
ROBO ANYTHING
ROCK OF THE 90'S
ROCKTOBER
ROCKUMENTARY
SHOP TIL YOU DROP
SIGNIFICANT OTHER
SOUND BITE
SPIN CONTROL
SPOKESMODEL
SUBTEXT
SUBVERSIVE
SUPERSTAR
SUPER ANYTHING

SURROUNDSOUND
SWATCH
SYNTHPOP
TELEVANGELIST
T.G.I.F.
A THOUSAND POINTS OF LIGHT
TOFUTTI
TRANCE CHANNELING
TRIVIAL PURSUIT
TUBULAR
ULTRA ANYTHING
VERNACULAR
VIDIOT
WACK
WACKO
WACKY
WANNABE
WILDING
WIRED
WORKAHOLIC
WUSS
YUPPIE
ZIP IT
ANYTHING IN HELL
ANYTHING IS HELL
ANYTHING FROM HELL

MORE FORBIDDEN WORDS
OF THE 1990s

ACTRESS/MODEL   AFFORDABLE   ALTERNATIVE ANYTHING
AROMATHERAPY   AS SEEN ON TV   AUDIOPHILE   AWARD-WINNING
BITE THE BIG ONE   BOTTOM LINE   BREAKFAST LINKS
THE CENTER FOR ANYTHING   CHILLIN'   COLD FUSION
COUCH POTATO   CRITICALLY ACCLAIMED   THE DARK KNIGHT
DESIGNER ANYTHING   DIFFERENT STROKES FOR DIFFERENT FOLKS
DOGBREATH   007   EARTH TO _____   EL LAY   ENERGIZER
FISHWICH   FLASHDANCE   GENIUS   GURU   HUNK   J.A.P.
I ♥ ANYTHING   I'M A SURVIVOR   KING OF ROCK 'N' ROLL
LIFE IN THE FAST LANE   LEGENDARY   LIMO   LITE ANYTHING
LIVING LEGEND   L-WORD   MCNUGGET   ME GENERATION
MEGABUCKS MEGADEATH   MEGA ANYTHING   MEN'S LIBERATION
MOVERS AND SHAKERS   NEOPSYCHEDELIC   NONREFUNDABLE
DEPOSIT   PARTY ANIMAL   PABULUM-PUKING LIBERALS   PUNDIT
PUNS ON THE WORD "FAX"   THE RIGHT STUFF   ROCK 'N' ROLL
HALL OF FAME   SEXPOLITATION   SMART ANYTHING   SMURF
SNEEZE GUARD   SPACE CADET   SPACE CASE   SPLATTER FILM
STREETWISE   SUPER MARIO BROS.   T&A   TACKY
THIRTYSOMETHING   ANY-NUMBER SOMETHING   THUMB'S DOWN
THUMB'S UP   STYLE   UNISEX   UPSIDE THE HEAD   VEEJAY
WHAT'S HOT (AND WHAT'S NOT)   WHERE'S THE BEEF?   WOODSTOCK
WOODSTOCK GENERATION   PRESIDENT QUAYLE

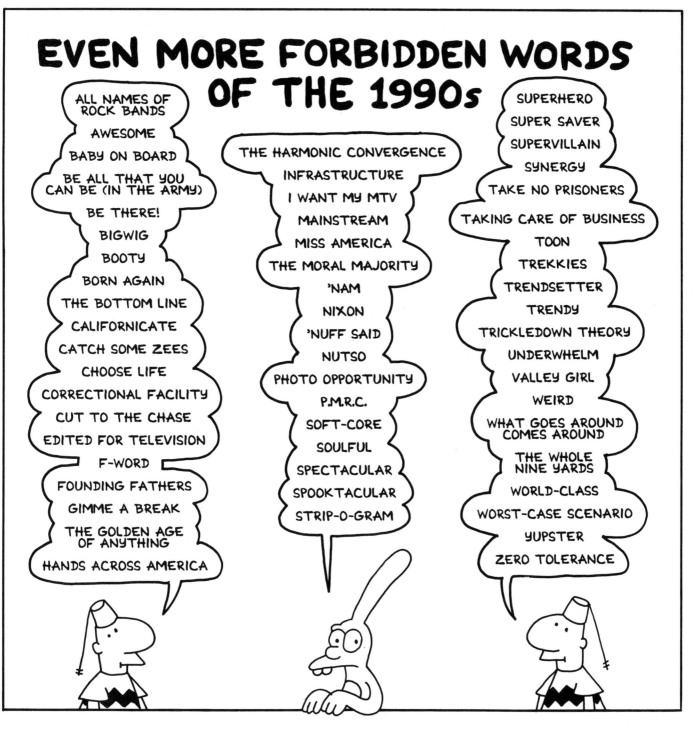

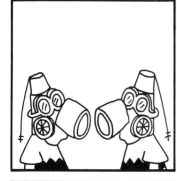
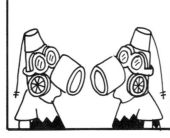

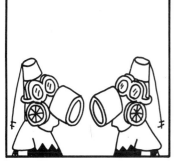

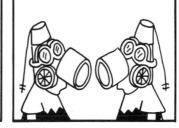
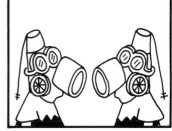
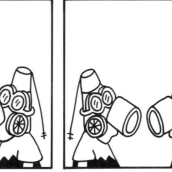
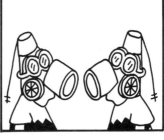
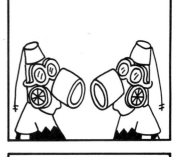
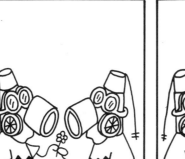